# NOT WITHOUT MY SON

Candy Jarrell

@@@@@@@@@@@@@@@

# Not Without My Son

@@@@@@@@@@@@@@

Candy Jarrell

First Printing: 2018

ISBN 978-1-387-53934-5

Candy Jarrell

P.O. BOX 251

Waxahachie, Texas 75168

www.candy,jarrell@rocketmail.com

I dedicate this book to all women that have suffered domestic abuse and single parents struggling to raise their children in a Godly fashion. May God give you strength, help, and power that will be a testimony to others that anything is possible through Christ.

"I can do all things through Christ which strengtheneth me."

(Philippians 4:13 (KJV))

# Table of Contents


Acknowledgments 5

Prologue 6 – 7

1. My Walk with Jesus 8 – 13
2. My Family 14 – 24
3. Good Choices for College, Bad Choices in Life 25 – 40
4. Goodbye USA – New Home Syria 41 – 48
5. Life in Aleppo 49 – 58
6. Weekends in Damascus 59 – 63
7. Living in Damascus 65 – 68
8. God Watches Me 69 – 72
9. Advancement & Freedom 74 - 85

Bibliography 86

# Acknowledgments

First, I want to give thanks to God for giving me the courage, strength, and His Holy Spirit to write this book. Also, I want to thank my son Gabriel for helping improve this book by providing excellent ideas and tips, and for putting up with all my exhausting questions. He is an excellent writer and I take his input very seriously. I also want to thank Emanuel for being there for me and my mother while she was alive. Both of my boys have blessed me tremendously by believing that I could succeed and have supported my efforts in the writing of this book. I love them both equally and deeply. I pray that this book will help many to trust in the Lord no matter what.

# Prologue

This book is about my struggles as a Christian growing up in a dysfunctional family that involved a history of poverty, mental illness, brokenness, domestic and incest abuse, and how through God's sovereign grace, I was able to overcome all of it. I also show through my experience a sharp contrast between not being evenly yoked in marriage vs. being evenly yoked in marriage.

From growing up as a Christian in Chicago, Illinois to living in Syria married to a Muslim who was abusive, to finally escaping his brutal attacks, I find my way back to where I should have been all along through God's guidance and His providence for my life.

When you read this book, it will seem as if I am writing a letter to my best friend. This is my writing style that I used because I take this book very personally since I am exposing my true self to the world. It was not easy for me to write this book because every time I had to add things to it or review it, it was as if I was re-living the events all over again. I cried many times recalling events that happened to my children and myself while writing this book. I have been trying to write this book ever since I divorced my husband since 1992. I started writing it in 1994 for therapeutic reasons at first, but then I just kept going.

This book is a love letter to all women everywhere that have suffered any kind of domestic abuse. I wrote this letter to proclaim to you that "not all is lost!" When you read this book, you will find out why.

Chapter One

# My Walk with Jesus

Since I was a baby, my grandmother and mom took me to The First Church of the Nazarene. There, I came to know about Jesus and was blessed with a deep spiritual love that has sustained me thus far. I accepted Jesus as my personal Savior at the age of five and was born again. I have clung to Him ever since.

I believe that Jesus died on the cross for our sins, and that He is the true Son of God, born of the Virgin Mary. I believe that the Father, Son, and Holy Spirit are one, and that They always existed in this form. I also believe that unless you accept Jesus into your heart and be spiritually born again, you can't enter the kingdom of heaven.

At the age of understanding (age twelve), I was baptized. You see, at the age of four I had accepted Him, but didn't have the knowledge yet of how to live my life according to His will. It was when I turned twelve that I had the Biblical knowledge and assertiveness to understand that it wasn't enough just to accept him, but I had to turn my life and soul over to Him, and I did just that.

It hasn't been an easy road, in fact, the life of all true Christians is very difficult because we must always put right before might. The hardest thing I've had to learn, in fact still learning, is to trust in the Lord. When you're poor, it's very hard to pay the tithe (10% of income) when you're supposed to. I know that when I am faithful, the Lord blesses me. Even when I don't pay my tithe because I felt unable financially and guilt fills my heart, He still looks after me and my children.

There were times when I knew I couldn't afford to pay my tithe and paid anyways. The Lord provided a way where I had money for the bills I needed to pay. A financial mistake is when I wrote out a check for tithe that I was unsure I could cover. Please folks, don't ever do this. It's embarrassing when you get a check returned to the church, and then must pay it back. Remember, God Himself doesn't need our money, for He has everything, but for the truth about Jesus to be known throughout the world, we need to realize that it costs a lot of money to do this. If every "Christian" in the world gave ten percent of their earnings, time, and energy into the work of Christ, I'm sure the world would know of Him, and eventually accept Him into their lives. No, I'm not trying to point any fingers. I'm just as guilty as the rest of you. I'm just pointing out a fact and hoping that these measures will be followed out. Remember, the Lord will not return unless His message is told to everyone, and I mean everyone!

My Lord Jesus is the only father I'd ever known and the best friend I've ever had. I only pray that others come to know Him as I have. His is the only true love, pure and innocent, without sin. He was the Lamb slain for our sins and is conqueror over death and evil. He fights our battles for us every day by the blood He has shed, the wounds He has sustained, and the pain He has endured. He loved us so much that He gave up His very life for us, even though we really weren't worth the price, He felt that we were worth it to Him. Yeah, we say we'd do the same for our children or loved one, but would you do it for a stranger or someone you hated? Jesus did this for all of us, even though we didn't deserve it. So, you see, God doesn't expect us to be perfect, because we can't be. We've fallen too far. But we can be perfect in

His eyes by coming to Jesus and confessing our sins, accepting Him as Lord and Savior, and communicating your heart to Him through prayer and supplications.

Traditional prayer is not what is meant by interpersonal relationship with God. It's OK for group prayer, but not OK when discussing personal matters with the Lord. You see, God wants you to express the real you, and wants you to pour your heart out to Him daily. Not only is this therapeutic in your case, but it gives God a chance to work in your life and perform miracles and interventions. God has a plan for each of our lives, but the tug of war that we all go through is from our refusal to let God's plan be carried out. You see, we think we know best and that we are doing the right thing, but it's totally the opposite from what God wants from us. We should come to be led by the Holy Spirit to things that seem contrary to our material wants and needs, and trust that He will provide. Bless be to God who gives me this knowledge and keeps it deep in my heart.

## Chapter Two

# My Family

My birth location in 1962 being Chicago, Illinois, is where I grew up. I lived in one of the poorest locations of the city in a basement apartment. I remember being a shy but playful little girl with blonde curly hair and bright blue eyes, that thought I was rich, even though I was very poor. I was raised by a strict, religious grandmother, and a mother who had mental illness. My father was not in my life growing up because my mother and father split up when I was only three months old.

I also remember picking up stray dogs and cats to bring home as pets and always being told "pets were not allowed", and I'd have to give them up, which always broke my heart, for I loved them and didn't want to give them up. We once kept a dog though with one blue eye and one brown eye for one week, but when the landlady found out, she told the landlord and said, "The pet would have to go.!" I cried my eyes out when they put him in the cage at the animal shelter and couldn't understand why things I loved were always taken away from me.

My mother was taken away from me when I was only seven years old. She pulled a knife on me, so my grandmother told me to run and hide. My grandma kept yelling, "Martha! Martha!", as she was trying to grab her arm that had the knife in it high up in the air. My mom then had to go to a mental hospital because of this mental break-down, so my grandmother was left to raise me.

Later in life I found out that her mental illness stemmed from the fact that she was molested and raped starting at the age of seven by her father. My grandmother contributed to her mental illness by blaming my mother for this and didn't protect her by leaving him. In those days, things like that were kept in the closet, and it was financially impossible for a woman who is uneducated to be financially independent to escape from that kind of situation. So, in a sense, my grandmother and mother were trapped with no way out except to live out their mascaraed lives, hoping that no one finds out.

On my father's side of the family, my real grandfather is not known because that secret went with my grandmother to her grave. I'll never know my real last name because my father was given his mother's maiden name, of which I use to have. This is a real problem for me because not only do I have a lost identity, but I also don't have an accurate medical history for hereditary diseases or a family history. My father took my two older brothers with him to Alabama to be raised by his mother and step-father when he separated from my mother. My brothers were raised on a farm while I was raised in the city. Even though we were apart, we kept in touch through letters and pictures.

The farthest back I can remember about my father is when I was three years old. I saw him from the attic window on Washtenaw Street in Chicago being handcuffed and arrested for trying to take me away from my mom and grandmother. I don't know why, but I can't remember anything else, and I couldn't see him very well. I remember crying because they were taking my dad away. He never wrote or paid child-support or visited afterwards.

At the age of fifteen I got to meet my brothers for the first time. Seeing them, I instantly recognized them as though I always knew them, even though we never actually grew up together. It was the most wonderful feeling, seeing them for the first time that mere words can't express. I always wished that we were never separated. I really feel that it was a tragedy that we were deprived of a childhood together. I loved them even though I never knew them.

The next time I saw my father was after coming home from Syria when I was twenty-seven years old. He looked a lot like my brother Ronnie, but only fatter. He had bright blue eyes, just like Ronnie's, a balding head, a pot belly, and only slightly taller than me, which surprised me because I had envisioned him a lot taller than that. He was wearing overalls and a plaid shirt and drove up in a red pick-up truck. He answered a lot of unanswered questions, but some of his answers I did not believe, especially when he denied some wrong doings of which my mother assured me were true. My mother was mentally ill (paranoid schizophrenia), but I know that she wouldn't lie about abuse. I did believe that he didn't cheat because my mother was very suspicious of him and accusative of doing these things (the paranoia part of my mother's condition).

When I came back from Syria, my mother's niece Ruby (my aunt Pearl DeRubis' daughter) told me a lot of things about my mother that I never knew before. She told me that she lived very promiscuously, drank a lot, and even took drugs when younger. It was then that I learned of the horrible things her father did to her. When she was only seven years old, her father molested and raped her. Also, I learned that when he was in Alabama, he had done the same thing to many of the girls in the family.

My grandmother at the time before their marriage was a desperate woman and was considered an "old maid" for her time and wasn't aware of her courter's past. You see, my grandmother was the oldest of twelve children and lived on a farm in Alabama. Her father was a share-cropper, so when her mother died, she had to take care of the rest of the children, so he could work. She was in her mid-thirty's when her father died, and so for survival reasons, she had to marry then. Mr. Davis, a widower with ten children, was convinced by his family to take her hand in marriage. As I understood from Ruby, they passed him off on her to get him away from the other girls that he was molesting and raping in the family, and possibly outside as well. What makes me so mad is that they knew all this the whole time and set my grandmother, and eventually, my mother up to be his next victims. He died, thank God, before I was born, or I would have been his next victim. Also, I remember my grandmother (may God rest her soul) telling me that she was raped before the age of twenty. I wonder if this had something to do with her not marrying sooner because of the way they thought back then of virginity, and of her being brought up in a strict religious environment. I personally think that her life was so unfair. She never got the chance to be loved by someone she wanted. Her life was basically a struggle to survive and taking care of others.

If it wasn't for my grandmother, I'd be dead today. She took care of me and my mom since we were born, and never turned her back on us. If there's one thing I've learned from her it's this – You don't give up on your loved ones, you must work hard to survive, and basically, DON'T GIVE UP AND RELY ON GOD.

She wasn't perfect though, and neither are any of us. I really believe that she was wrong in not protecting her daughter (my mom) from her dad. If I had a daughter, and someone did that to her, I guarantee you that I would do everything in my power to prevent that from happening again. She blamed her and said that she had acted promiscuously, at seven years old? No wonder she had a mental break-down! How would you feel if most of your life your own mother thought of you as a slut, ignored claims of rape, and then say it's your own fault, and she won't believe you, even if she suspects it to be true when you tell her about it? The fear of survival or pride, or whatever it was that possessed my grandmother not to do anything about this situation should never have kept her from protecting her own daughter. I've come to forgive her though. You must in order to go on with your life. You can't expect God to forgive you if you can't forgive others, though I find it very difficult to ever forgive my grandfather for what he did to my mother. My mother at this very moment (11/29/1995) is in a hospital psych ward, still suffering from the past, and I blame her father. Even though I never knew him, and he's dead, his spirit still haunts her and keeps her from living a normal life.

Last time she was committed to a mental institute was when I was seven years old. She was raped in it and constantly drugged and given shock treatments. I do not trust these places for her because all have criminals in them that are dangerous, and she is not. She just has a problem with understanding how to manage her life and needs someone to help her, just like we all eventually will. She also needs to know that someone is there that loves and cares for her. Does this sound abnormal? Some people can live by themselves and do just fine, while others will struggle to survive and get easily depressed. My mother is the later, but in the extreme sense. I am not saying she isn't mentally ill. What I am saying is that she is better off with me, not living in my house, but nearby, and she'll be all right. The reason I'd never having her live in my house is my children would make her very nervous, and we don't get along. I love my mother, but she has these mood swings and cusses and says nasty things in front of my children that I'd never allow.

I was expecting my mother to spend Thanksgiving with us here in Arkansas. I would take the plane to visit her in Illinois and thought it would be nice to send her a plane ticket to visit us here instead. Instead of visiting for Thanksgiving, she was hospitalized for seeing snakes because she had not been taking her medication. I wanted to bring her here to stay in Arkansas, but she wanted to stay with her friends. Her "friends" committed her to a mental ward of the hospital, which would have never had to be if she had someone to monitor her every day, which I would have done if she were here.

Chapter Three

# Good Choices for College, Bad Choices in Life

When I was eight years old I went to Salem Evangelical Church in Chicago for a while. I liked it there because they had children's activities and clubs that helped me learn about the Bible and got me active amongst other Christians my age. Here I was involved in the AWANA and CHUMS clubs. They even had Catechism every Wednesday after school that brought children into the Word of God that otherwise would have never heard it. Here, I met Evelyn Dennison, a missionary that was assigned to Africa. I remember winning a contest and she showed me all over Moody Bible Institute in Chicago. She also showed me where she lived there. It was very nice and looked like a beautiful hotel. One day we were sitting in church services and she said, "I don't know why I'm telling you this, but God told me you'd be traveling far away to another country when you get older." Well, being from a poor family and never had traveled outside of Chicago, I thought she had lost her mind, or I had just misunderstood what she had said. Now I know she wasn't crazy for she was prophesizing to me what I would encounter. When I think back on it, the way she told me she seemed troubled in telling me about it, like it was a type of warning with this vision. She was foretelling my journey that would take me to Syria.

In my journey growing up, I always wanted to be a doctor. When I had split my baby toe in two and had to wear a cast for three months, I was very grateful to my physical therapist that got me through it. Also, there was a Sunday school teacher named

Helen Laymen that had severe arthritis and had to be in a wheelchair. She had to have many surgeries and eventually could use a walker. She was a very intelligent woman and I admired her greatly. I prayed for her every day as a child and noticed her improvement. It is mainly because I wanted to see her get better is what drove me to want to be a physical therapist.

I started out my curriculum by attending Wright Jr. College in Chicago. Here is where I took most of my pre-requisites, and here is where I met my first husband Nazar. The first time I saw him was in the college cafeteria. He was wearing yellow dress-pants and a dress-shirt. To me he resembled a banana. I was talking to my girlfriend at the time. We were discussing Arab Muslim women wearing the cover. I was laughing at how ridiculous it was, and how they can't see where they are going. I was making fun of them bumping into things as they were walking. He apparently found this all too amusing, so he decided to come over to our table. He tried to explain to me why women wore the cover for religious reasons. I just proceeded to persuade him how ridiculous it all was, and eventually he even agreed on some of it. He thought it stupid that he couldn't even see his own cousins, and because of it, doesn't recognize them when they visit. I found him a little weird at first, but then came to like him. He looked to me like an Arab version of John Claude Van Dame, which at the age of twenty, was very appealing.

Our first date was in the winter at Chicago's Art Institute. I had to do a paper for Humanities class, so I suggested that we have lunch there. It was freezing out and I didn't have enough warm clothes on. He had the audacity to ask me to take a stroll with him near the lake. I agreed, but because it was cold, only for a short while. Well, he took me for a great distance and then we sat on a bench. It was freezing mind you, and he proceeded to kiss me and get a little too fresh. At first, I liked him kissing me, but then he proceeded to unbutton my blouse and wouldn't let me go. I got very angry and told him to stop. He finally got control of his senses and proceeded to walk me back to the museum. We then went home our separate ways. I decided that I didn't want to see him any more after that, so I told him at school that I couldn't see him any longer. I was the president of the Chess Club at Wright Jr. College and wrote a message on the board that I'd thought he'd understand to tell him it was over. Apparently, he didn't get it.

A year later he called my house to ask me out again. I explained to him that I had made a mistake dating a Muslim, and that I should only date Christians. Well, he sounded so pitiful on the phone, I felt sorry for him and agreed to only talk to him at a chess club meeting I was having at Northeastern Illinois University, of which I had become president of. I was training as a nurse's assistant at the time and was dressed in my uniform and lab jacket. I had no time to change and a chess tournament was going on. I had to make him wait until the games were over before I could talk to him. He told me that he still was thinking of me and wanted to go out with me. I still told him that my beliefs were contrary to his and that it would not be a good idea. He told me that he was lonely and needed someone just to talk to. I said it was OK if we remained just friends.

He asked me out to a movie, and that's where it started. He took me after the movie to a part of the theater that had no audience, and there he told me he loved me, and proceeded to kiss me passionately where he almost took my breath away. I knew that I was starting to fall in-love and my head was spinning. Afterwards, we spent as much time together as possible.

He was a student also and was renting a room form Mrs. Laughlin in Oak Park. It was the summer of 1984 that she went on vacation. As soon as he knew she was gone, we spent time together there. He lived on the second floor. When he first brought me upstairs to his room, I was a bit apprehensive. I cried and prayed and asked the Lord to forgive me for what I was about to do. I knew what I was going to do would be wrong, but I loved this man and just wanted to be with him, and knew I had to be.

He asked me on bended knee on June 1984 at Buckingham fountain in Chicago to marry him. I said "yes" and the rest is history. We got married on September 1st, 1984 at Cook County Court House and had a Hawaiian reception in a rented hall with a live band. Many of my best friends, co-workers, and family were there. I had a hard time getting my grandmother and mother to come to the reception because they didn't approve of the marriage. My friends finally convinced them to come and made me the happiest bride when I saw them. They were right but knew that I had to learn for myself that this was a mistake.

We rented an apartment in Oak Park and really couldn't afford to live there. I remember encouraging him to call his father to tell him we were married. He called Syria long-distance on a pay phone at the laundromat. He lied to me, telling me he had told his father, and I even tried speaking to them, but they didn't speak English, and I didn't speak Arabic, so I didn't know what was being said. He made me think they understood me but didn't. He also told me that his father would send $10,000, but he never did. He eventually admitted that he lied about that. He made himself out to be something he wasn't. I'd have much rather preferred honesty over lies and false hopes any day.

When I was about 3 months pregnant, I found out who the real Nazar was. While I was cooking breakfast, he started pinching my bottom hard. I told him to stop, but he decided to do it again. By an instant reflex, I slapped him as hard as I could. Suddenly, he flew into a rage, slapping me and dragging me by my hair and kicking me. I found myself laying on the doorway of our bedroom, trying to keep myself from miscarrying. When he came to his senses, he helped me up. I went directly to the closet, got out my suitcase, and proceeded to pack. He was begging me not to leave him and that he'd never do it again. At first, I didn't listen to him, but then he assured me that this incident would never be repeated. Now that I look back on the incident, I wished that I had left then, for history repeated itself to the point where I felt there was no way out.

Because I was pregnant, we knew we had to move to something more affordable. We lucked out when we found this place in Berwyn. It was a huge 2-bedroom apartment, hardwood floors, and beautiful shade trees all around. The only problem was it had no yard, but the area was good and clean. Nazar and I eventually helped my grandmother and mom out of a bad area of Chicago and moved them into a nice apartment in Cicero.

I worked at Courtesy Home Center part-time in Forest Park until our baby was born on June 11th, 1985. I went into the hospital on June 10th, but the baby didn't come. Nazar slept at Cook County Hospital in Chicago, expecting to see the baby when he woke up, but I still was in labor. The baby didn't come until 8:00 pm the next day. A beautiful baby boy, 8lbs 14oz., which we named Mohamed Gabriel, was born. The reason we named him Gabriel is because Gabriel was the only religious being we agreed upon, and that being he is the messenger of God.

When we took him home we didn't have a crib. Nazar refused to spend a lot of money on a crib, so he found a TV table that someone had thrown out and made a crib out of it. I'll never forget it. It had a swinging door that swung up and closed by 2 nails that flipped up on each side. To me it was more of a coffin than a crib. Yes, folks, he was that cheap. My friends and relatives bought a lot of my baby's clothes and other needs, thank God, or I'm afraid he would have hunted in the garbage for that too.

The second abusive incident I remember is when he was laying on the bed in our bedroom reading a book. I remember getting in an argument with him over something and then seeing him throw a book at me, which landed on my left hip. There was a huge bruise on my hip for weeks and it felt as if my hip was broken.

During our marriage, he was still practicing his religion. He would pray every now and then in the Muslim tradition on a little rug. He once asked me to try praying his way, and so to please him, I tried it. I found myself laughing so hard while trying, I was beside myself. I just couldn't do it. I was used to only praying the Christian way and felt uncomfortable praying this weird way. He was angry inside that I refused to pray his way.

On January of 1986 when the space craft "Challenger" went down, the worst day of my life coincided with this tragedy. We had a black and white TV at home and we were very concerned about this event. Nazar suggested that we go to my grandmother and mother's house to see it on their colored TV. My mother, being nervous, got tired of us staying too long and asked us to leave. Nazar had the baby in his arms and got very angry at her for saying this. He said, "How dare you ask us to leave after we helped you move out of a bad apartment into this much better area!" My grandmother thought that he was going to hit my mom, so she stepped in front of my mother, doubled up her fists and said, "You better not hurt my daughter!" Nazar then took his hand and pushed her by her forehead, causing her to fly across the floor, landing on her bottom. A streak of hatred for him cut through my heart, for she was 84 years old and the only person who truly loved and cared for me. I went to her and asked if she was all right. She said she was and to look out for the baby. I didn't want to leave her, but when I saw Nazar with the baby, I was afraid that he'd run off with him, so I followed him to the car. When we arrived at home, police cars were standing by waiting to arrest him. When they hand-cuffed him, they put me in the other squad-car and asked me questions about the incident. I told them the truth.

They put him in jail and I went to see him. He was crying, and I felt sorry for him. I had no other means of support and I was worried about the baby, so I agreed to help him get out. I went to his bail hearing which was set at $5,000. I had to come up with $500, so I told his bank about the situation, and they let me sign for him. I paid the bail to get him out but found out afterwards that the trial had reached the papers, so there would likely be a larger sentence than originally hoped for.

I told Nazar the truth about what the lawyers had said the out-come of the case would be. They said that the sentence would be 2 years with no possibility of parole. He hadn't had any previous record and wondered why such a stiff sentence. Then I read the newspaper article which made the public know that that he was an Arab Muslim and gave a detailed report of the incident. Then I put 2 and 2 together and realized that the sentence was high because the public blew this incident out of proportion because of who he was. I myself knowing the sentence to be too high and unfair, suggested that he go back to Syria. I was mainly worried that that he'd be a target in prison from homosexuals and perverts because in the Chicago prison system, there are high incidents of this kind. He was literally terrified, so he decided to go back to Syria, and that I'd follow him latter with our son Gabriel.

The day he left for Syria was one of the saddest and scariest times of my life. I remember kissing him goodbye with tears streaming down both of our faces, and the baby crying. I waved goodbye and was sitting on the bench to the el-train terminal to O'Hare Airport wondering what I was going to do without my husband. I cried all the way home. When I reached home, I decided to sell everything in the house to make the money for the plane ticket to Syria. I advertised in the newspaper, and by the end of February I had most of the items sold.

## Chapter Four

# Goodbye USA - New Home Syria

I bought a ticket to leave at the end of February and then proceeded to get my visa. I had never traveled outside of the country before, so I didn't know what to do. Well, I had gotten all my paperwork in order in time. I was paranoid that I'd be stopped at the airport because of my husband's record, so I asked a friend that I knew to go with me to the airport. I'll never forget it. I was scared to death, wearing a white rabbit fur coat, and carrying a lot of luggage, including trunks.

I said goodbye to my friend and my country and proceeded to board the plane. I remember looking out the plane window crying and wondering if I'd ever see my country again. I couldn't believe that this was happening to me. I was recalling saying goodbye to my grandma and mom in their apartment. I lied to them, telling them I was just moving and needed to borrow a trunk for moving. I was afraid to tell them I was leaving the country, for I knew they would try to stop me. I kissed my grandma last, and that was the last time I literally saw her on this earth. Less than 2 months later the Lord took her home. Sometimes I wonder if I was partially to blame for her death, for she loved me a lot and might have lived longer if I was there to take care of her. I loved my grandmother more than anyone on this earth and hope she forgave me for all the trouble I had caused her.

My flight took over 18 hours plus a lay-over. I took Alia airlines to Amman, Jordan for a day lay-over. The next day I flew to Damascus, Syria.

My Gabriel was 7 months old at the time and had a scar from a burn on his left arm that was healing. Oh, I forgot to mention how he got the scar. Well, before the trip, I had to still work at Courtesy Home Center to survive, so I hired a baby-sitter upstairs from me to look after him while I worked. She had the radiators on full-blast because it was cold. She put my baby on the bed instead of the crib. She said that he kicked himself from under the covers and caught his arm in the radiator. He was rushed to the hospital before I came home from work.

I went to pick my baby up from the babysitter and I said, "Where's my baby?" A girl who was not the babysitter, but another neighbor told me what had happened, and I ran out to the street screaming, "My baby, my baby, God no!" A friend drove up and asked what happened. I told them, and they drove me to the hospital.

When I reached the hospital, I saw my baby in an oxygen tent with plastic all around his bed. I couldn't even touch him. I just heard him crying out so pitifully that it cut right through my heart. I was literally in shock. The next day I had to hold my baby down as the surgeon pulled the dead skin off my baby's arm while hearing him screaming. After this, I quit my job and just got ready to go to Syria. I still had to change the bandages on my baby's arm after the trip for a week. He recovered, but it left a scar all the way up his left arm.

When I arrived in Damascus I was instantly in culture shock. When I looked all around me all I saw was people dressed in black. It was like seeing a huge funeral procession and being in the center of it.

I was met by my husband and two of his brothers, Mustafa and Taher. I was wearing a silk royal-purple dress and walked up to them with my baby in the stroller (who was asleep). Nazar was surprised that I came and was happy to see me. We had to take a bus to Aleppo which was a four-hour trip. I was greeted warmly at the door by Noora (the youngest and prettiest sister) who hugged and kissed me on both cheeks. It is customary to kiss the father-in-law on his hand and put it to my head three times, which I did. It was real hard for me to get use to this custom. Another thing that was hard to get use to was listening to the "Allah ou Akbars" which means "God is greater" on the loud speakers five times every day at dawn, midday, afternoon, sunset and night. It took me a whole month to adjust to that craziness.

The next sister I met was Ghada. Her and I became best friends as time went on, for she is the one who taught me Arabic, and I taught her English. She was not physically attractive, but had a nice personality, and was a hard, loyal, and dedicated worker. She took over for her mother (surprisingly just as my grandmother did for her mother) when her mother died.

Their mother died one year before we were married. They didn't bother to tell Nazar until 4 months after we were married. When they had sent him a letter, indicating her death, he tried to kill himself with a knife, and I took the knife out of his hand, and kept him from committing suicide. I felt as if his mother's spirit sensed his pain and spoke to me to make sure he eats, so I cooked him something I knew he liked, spaghetti. He eventually ate and felt better. I don't let these experiences control me. I just go on and give God the glory for whatever it means and don't worry about it, for God is my guide and I need not worry for anything.

At first the family accepted me, but when they realized that I was a true Christian and wasn't willing to become a Muslim, they started to turn on me. Nazar was required to be in the Syrian army for two and a half years, so I had to live with my in-laws in Aleppo. The aunts would come over wearing a scarf over their heads as a show of disrespect for me being a Christian in their household. You see, the custom is usually to take off their scarf in front of women, but they felt I wasn't good enough to see their hair. You think, now why should that bother you? Why should you care what their hair looks like? Well, at first, I didn't, until I found out the meaning of what they were doing to me. It's like a big insult and rejection being thrown in your face.

Also, the family use to pray in Islamic fashion in front of me until Mustafa's wife refused to pray in my presence. Then, they followed her example. This made my husband Nazar very angry, and he told her off. I told Nazar that I didn't care where she prayed. It wouldn't make any difference anyways. I'd always be a Christian.

Finally, my father-in-law got mad at Nazar for something and called our son Gabriel a "kahen (priest/preacher), which made Nazar very angry. Well, I answered Fahker (my father-in-law) by saying, "En-Sha Allah," meaning "God willing." Well this really set him off, and then I knew we were never going to get along.

## Chapter Five

# Life in Aleppo

Our first romantic trip in Syria was going to Latakia which is a sea-port where oil tankers fill up. There were beautiful grape vineyards and orchards of fruit trees, and the beach had white sand. I noticed a Texaco oil tanker with an American flag on it near the shore. We had a very wonderful time there eating a picnic and enjoying the scenery. When we arrived back to Aleppo, Nazar received a notice that he was to be enlisted into the Syrian Army.

When Nazar went to the army, he was only on leave one weekend out of a month, so I hardly got to see him. I was under enough tension with my in-laws but having to be without my husband felt almost unbearable. I had to learn to eat their way, cook their way, and clean their way.

They got me up early in the morning to do chores, they cooked everything by hand, and they had no toilet paper or paper towels. It was like living in hell. It was my worst nightmare come true. I felt like Cinderella that never finds the glass slipper.

When doing the laundry, I couldn't go out to the balcony to hang up the clothes without a scarf. When hanging up the clothes, I had to hide the underwear in the back of the other clothes, so no one would see them. This took the underclothes a lot longer to dry, and because of not being directly exposed to the sun, a lot less sanitary. The diapers were cloth and had to be washed by hand in a barrel, boiled in hot water, and then put in the washing machine (which was the old type with the wringer). Ghada helped me a lot with this, for I couldn't do it alone.

Cooking the Arab way was sort of an adventure. The whole family of women would get together after shopping for vegetables, or picking pistachios in the field, and we'd gather around a big table and process the food. This would take all day.

When there is an event or family gathering, it's much worse. They would cook all kinds of kibbe' and yogurt soup and might even slaughter a ram right there in the kitchen. We'd also scrape out and stuff eggplant and zucchini with rice, meat, and pine-nuts. They also make a pancake fried in butter on one side called "siyalet" that they'd sprinkle cinnamon sugar on and roll it up to eat.

Another dessert was "kinafe" that is stringed filo dough fried in butter and then sprinkled with cinnamon sugar. There are too many dishes to name, but you get the general idea. Everything was made by hand, and every woman was required to know how to cook well to fit into their system.

It took me a while to learn how to eat with Arabic bread (khubz), which is like our pita bread, but tastes much better. You see, in the Middle-East we don't eat with utensils but pick everything up with khubz. We usually put all the different foods in dishes or small bowls on a large round serving tray (sanea) and we place this tray in the middle of the rug. The whole family would gather around the rug to eat. The foods usually eaten would be olives (black and/green), a jam/preserve (usually apricot (mish-mush), a chick-pea dip (hummus), olive oil (zate zatoon), a sesame-seed oily paste like peanut butter (tahini), sesame seeds (zater), and a sweet crumbly peanut/sesame candy (haloway). The main thing I didn't like about this type of eating is the fact that we dipped from the same bowls, which to me is unsanitary. Remember, there is no toilet paper.

Cleaning was the biggest hassle of all. Did you know that you must wash the whole house every day because of the environmental conditions, the house gets dustier quicker? We don't use a mop to wash floors as I do in the U.S. but use a huge squeegee and a hose to wash the floors. There are drains in certain areas of the house where the water goes down.

We also wash the walls by hosing them down and dust all the furniture by beating the chairs and couches with a big rag to get the dust out. Then sometimes we must make our own mattresses by stuffing heavy material with wool, and then sew up all the way around like a huge pillow. At other times, we must cover old/new quilts with fancy material and sew around it by hand. Then at other times we must wash wool by hand and hang it over the balcony railing to dry.

My father-in-law is in the business of selling sheep (ghunam), so we always have plenty of wool and meat. He and his brothers own over 2,000 sheep and have a large quantity of land. His mother and father use to be poor, until his father decided to sell all the gold they had to buy a large quantity of land in Aleppo. He raised sheep for a living and grew many pistachio trees. The family became famous for the best sheep and pistachio's in the Middle East, and thus began their dynasty.

Their name is known throughout Syria and the family keeps growing. I have kept their last name out of the book because even though I had a hard time with my husband, it's no reason to drag the family's name through the mud. Even though I had problems with them, I still love them, but I decided to keep my distance for the sake of my children and our safety. I just wish for peace and understanding among me and their family and wish them no harm. I pray that someday they would come to know Jesus as I have, and know that it is not through works, but by the blood of Jesus that they're even able to approach the throne of God. Please listen and hear what the Spirit is saying to you through this book and maybe you'll get the answers to the questions you've been searching your whole life for.

Now let me set the scene for exactly who I was living with in that household, and the relatives not living there as well. Fahker was my father-in-law and was the supreme head of the household. Nazar (my husband) was the oldest son (currently in the army). Mustafa was next to the oldest son and training to run the family business (selling sheep). Taher was next in line. Malek was an athletic teenager who liked to play soccer. Braheem was a sweet 12-year-old boy who basically missed his mom. Nahed was the oldest sister, in fact, older than Nazar. She was married to a super-religious, educated and prosperous man who lived in his own house not far from ours. Nahed was the socialite of the family. Nidah was the 2nd oldest sister and younger than Nazar. She married a veterinarian, which in Syria, doesn't make much money. He was always trying to squeeze money out of my father-in-law. They also had their own house. Ghada was the next oldest and unmarried. Her duties were to take care of the household. Noora was the youngest and prettiest sister who fought a lot with Ghada over the household chores.

One day, Noora got into the usual argument with Ghada about who's supposed to do what in the house. The problem was that Nazar was on leave from the army and heard them arguing. He picked up a broom and started hitting Noora over the head repeatedly. I told him to stop. When he didn't, I hit him on the arm and yelled, "Stop!" Then I went back into the kitchen to cook lunch. He ran into the kitchen after me and started beating me up. His brothers had to pull him off me. He was in his own country now and felt he could do that and get away with it, and you know, he did!

There are no laws what-so-ever to protect women, and even if there were, they're not enforced. The family won't let you do anything about it, in fact, they accept this kind of behavior, in fact, expect it from their male relatives. They think that their image is more important than anything and wish to preserve that facade. They are living in a hypocritical illusion that just seems to never end.

They call themselves followers of God, and yet allow such things to go on. Shame on them! How dare they call themselves Godly when they don't even know what that means. Wake up to reality! See things as they truly are! Stop hiding behind your mask and admit the truth! Take a self-examination of yourself and ask, "Am I doing the right thing?" If not, ask yourself; "What can I do to make it right?" Well, I got the answer for you. **CHANGE!** Change from the way you treat women and accept them as equal in everything. We are human beings, not animals! We have feelings the same as you, a mind the same as you, and a God-given spirit the same as you. Stop it! Stop it now before the judgment of the Almighty God be upon each one of your heads!

## Chapter Six

# Weekends in Damascus

Eventually, I rented a room in an ancient Christian village in Damascus so that I would have a place to stay while I taught English as a second language on the weekends. Damascus is where I heard stories concerning the truth about Muhammad and how he received his message. I was told that Muhammad wanted to conquer Palestine, so he sent a spy to find out about the people and their beliefs. The spy came back and told him everything that he had written down of what he had learned from his visit. Muhammad chopped off the spy's head. The information written was used as his words, rather than that of Jesus' or of the disciples. Muhammad also had epilepsy, which was not understood in that time-period. When the people witnessed him having one of his seizures, they thought he was having a vision.

I was also told that when Muhammad went to the door of a Christian family's home, a woman dressed in her sheer-looking night clothes answered the door. Well, Muhammad considered this seeing the woman naked and felt that under God's law that he had to marry her. So, he made the husband divorce his wife in order so that he could have a legal marriage ceremony. Then Muhammad returned her to her husband where they had to get married over again.

The main difference between Jesus and Muhammad is Jesus wasn't a warrior or a conqueror of lands, nor ever killed anyone while on the earth. He was a man of peace. Muhammad, on the other hand, was out for power and glory, and to accomplish this, he had to win over his people by making himself out to be something he wasn't. Hmmm, doesn't that phrase sound familiar? Muhammad himself might have truly thought he was a prophet and a God-sent, but he wasn't. He was a good military leader that helped conquer land for his people. He was the ultimate general but used deceptive tactics. If he was truly a man of God, why did he have so many wives, killed so many times, and sounded like the Bible in all his so-called prophesies? You know where Muhammad is buried, but do you know where Jesus is? Why are you revering a dead man? Why not revere the one who's alive?

I was travelling alone on the bus from Damascus to go home to Aleppo. This was one of the cheaper busses called "Hope-Hope Bus" and called this because a person would call out "hope! hope!" to stop the bus. Plus, this bus would stop for anyone, anywhere.

Well, when the bus stopped in a remote area, they picked up a soldier and he was carrying a rifle. He asked the bus driver, “Wano ejnabeya?” which means “Where is the foreigner?” He proceeded to sit down right next to me with the rifle in between us.

As the bus proceeded, the bus driver turned off the lights, and being night time, it was very dark. I then felt a hand on my leg and realized what was happening. I was scared to death and was afraid he would shoot me.

When he tried to put his hand on my leg again, I screamed and stood up in the bus and said something in a foreign language (that I did not know), all the while trying to grab for his throat. The bus driver made the soldier sit behind me next to this man, and I sat next to the man’s wife. I was terrified.

When we came to a stop, the bus driver and others asked me if I was a Muslim. I said "yes" because I was terrified that they wouldn't protect me from this man if I said otherwise. Directly afterwards, my conscience pricked me like never before, and it felt as though the Lord's Spirit left me.

Why didn't I tell them the truth? Aren't I supposed to be stronger than that? I had a hard time forgiving myself for that, but eventually realized that St. Peter did the same thing. He was weak and so was I. Even he came to realize that he wasn't as strong as he made himself out to be. Neither are we all.

I wish that I'd been stronger and wished that I could have taken it back and corrected the mistake, but the past is done, and it can't be changed. That is why we as Christians should be very careful in our thinking that we can always be strong as Christians, because we can’t. it is our humanity that always gets in the way. Lord God forgive us for we are weak creatures and need your forgiveness to see us through.

## Chapter Seven

# Living in Damascus

When I decided that I needed to be totally out of my in-law's house and closer to my husband (as he served in the military), I moved out to live on the mountain of Rouknaldeen in Damascus. I lived in a house literally carved out of the mountain with wooden logs as a roof. There, I had to heat water on a Bunsen burner, which occasionally got clogged, so I had to use a needle (nicashay) to open the nozzle.

My husband hooked up our electricity to the neighbors once without telling them, and boy did the neighbor get a shock when he received the bill. The neighbor called the police when he realized what he had done and threatened to put him in jail. My husband eventually agreed to pay half the bill to settle the dispute.

It was on this mountain that I started to get symptoms from my gall-bladder disease. I would have sharp pains that came right in the middle, but below my chest area. It felt like knives being stuck in my gut, and then feeling the knives twisting. I had gotten so bad that I had tried to kill myself by overdosing on pain medication. Before I could take the rest of the bottle, something stopped my hand and told me to stop. I listened and lay on the bed to sleep off the high dose I took (8 pills). I'm really surprised that that didn't kill me. I knew that this was an angel or Jesus himself that stopped me from killing myself. I am grateful I didn't, for later in life I was to have another beautiful baby boy.

Living on this mountain was the most challenging experience of my life. I had to walk down this very steep mountain every day to get vegetables, fruit, and meat. There was this shop that made hummus every morning. All the children were sent there to get it for their families early every morning.

Farmers would display their goods on burlap rugs or in baskets, and we'd bend down to see what was suitable enough to buy. There were also shops that ran along the mountain and below it that sold a variety of goods. Most shops specialized in a particular item or food.

One of my favorite places to go was the dairy shop that sold all kinds of cheeses, yogurts, and ice creams. There were no American cheeses or aged yellow or orange cheeses like in the US, but their cheeses were white, sweet, and freshly made. Some were stringed, twisted, and braided with poppy seeds. Others were square and were preserved in salt water.

There was another place that sold only milk. Here, they made the cheeses and other milk products that the store sold. People would wait in line with bowls and pitchers for the fresh, hot milk. You see, most people that lived on the mountain had no refrigerators, so they had to do things day by day.

Chapter 8

# God Watches Me

I used to go to Sheik Ramadan in Damascus and have had long discussions with him about the Holy Bible and the Koran. I was not afraid to tell this man about Jesus, even though I knew I was the only one there that believed in Him. I was not paid as a missionary, nor was I told by anyone to do this. I just stood up for what I believed in and told Sheik Ramadan what I believed to be the truth. He also told me what he believed to be true and gave arguments of why he thought the Holy Bible was a false doctrine. I told him there was no way on this earth I would ever accept Islam, and he told me the same for Christianity.

There was a multitude of women present during this discussion and a translator, so many heard what I proclaimed to them that I believed Mohammad to be a false prophet. I just hope that I got some of them thinking about what I had said and pray that the Holy Spirit works in their lives. I only wish good for this people and am concerned about their spiritual welfare. I am harsh in my words to you in this fashion, not because of anything my husband has done. I am speaking directly to the Muslim people.

There is a mosque that I had visited in Damascus, the Umayyad Mosque, in which I had felt very strange in. I felt a sense of familiarity. Later I was to find out that this mosque was previously a church and was taken over by the Muslims in war. I had also found that the head of John the Baptist was in a crypt there.

The Muslims call him "Yahya." Matthew 14:12: "John's disciples came and took his body and buried it." "The Gospels do not say where John was buried. In the time of Julian, the Apostate, however, his tomb was shown at Samaria, where the inhabitants opened it and burned part of his bones. Some Christians, who carried them to an abbot of Jerusalem named Philip, saved the rest."[1] "Shi'a Muslim tradition maintains that the head of John the Baptist is interred in the once-called Basilica of Saint John the Baptist[2], which is now the Umayyad Mosque in Damascus, Syria."[3] "Pope John Paul II visited the tomb of John the Baptist at the Umayyad Mosque during his visit to Syria in April, 2001."[4]

Another strange thing happened to me that only assures me that God is watching me. I had been

[1] http://www.newworldencyclopedia.org/entry/John_the_Baptist
[2] https://en.wikipedia.org/wiki/Beheading_of_St._John_the_Baptist
[3] http://www.newworldencyclopedia.org/entry/John_the_Baptist
[4] https://en.wikipedia.org/wiki/Beheading_of_St._John_the_Baptist

teaching English to a little boy in Damascus on the 1st floor of a building, when a lady from the 3rd floor came down to speak to me. She was a Moslem woman, but the boy's family I was teaching was Christian.

She said, "I know you. I know your mother. She showed me pictures of your wedding." I looked up at her totally astonished and wondered what else she knew about me. Suddenly I had gotten really scared, thinking she knew what my husband had done and would tell this family. Also, I was embarrassed thinking that she knew of my mother's poverty and mental condition.

She said that my mother would go into her son's store and buy things from them. My mother became friends with her and even invited her to her house. This wealthy woman visited my mother and I was totally flabbergasted. A woman in Damascus, Syria knows my mother and this woman I had never met before. This to me was too much of a coincidence and just proved to me that there was no such thing as coincidence.

Chapter Nine

# Advancement & Freedom

My private tutoring ESL (English as a Second Language) business became popular in Damascus and led to important jobs such as speech and letter writing for an Argentinian UN major who accepted the Nobel peace prize in Damascus, as well as working for majors in the United Nations that worked for the Argentinian Embassy. Also, I once worked tutoring a prince from the United Emirates, but when I laughed at his pronunciation, he fired me. I also taught children of doctors and important Christian business families. The Syrian Government hired me to teach a Communications Class for Bankers in Damascus. I was even offered to head up the English Department at the University of Damascus, but because I only had an Associate Degree at that time, they couldn't hire me. Eventually, I taught at ICARDA in Aleppo, Syria in an elementary school, focusing on a down's syndrome child.

While living in Aleppo, my father-in-law (Fahker) said that he gave us a house, but it was in my brother-in-law's name (Taher), and he did not bother to tell me this until after I had paid out of my own money to paint the interior of the house with many coats of expensive paint, as well as fixing the house up. Fahker did help me out a lot when I first came to Syria, so I did not make a fuss over it, however, it did make me very angry.

While living there, Gabriel was 3 years old and very mischievous. He almost ruined everything in the house after we painted by turning the petrol heater dial on high, causing flames to spew everywhere. He even caught the Christmas tree on fire and Nazar had to throw it out of the window to keep the rest of the house from burning. You see, we had a stone building, so the house itself won't burn down, but it can be damaged from the inside, or blow up if too much petrol is spilled from a heater.

Also, Gabriel decided to sneak out of the house one day. A shepherd came to my door and told me that my son was riding on one of his sheep like it was a horse and wanted me to take my son home. I went after him and gave him a lecture and a swat on his bottom. I was just glad he was not kid-napped and alive.

When Nazar got out of the military, he decided to ask his father if we could go back to the United States so that he could make more money. He said yes, but because he had a record, I would have to go first to make sure that he would not be arrested when he got off the plane. I had to leave my son Gabriel there in Syria to do this.

I decided to ask my brother Ronnie if I could live with him in Alabama. He said yes, and that is where I did my research and phone calls from to see if there was still a warrant out for his arrest. I found out that the case was thrown out of court and that he could come back.

Then, I asked my father's step-father for $1000 to send to my husband to come here in exchange for me keeping the house clean and helping him out. I sent it to my husband and then he came with our son Gabriel. Then, I worked as a nurse's assistant at Hellen Keller Hospital in Sheffield, Alabama. My cousin was the head-nurse of the hospital and was married to one of the chiefs of staff (who was a leading doctor). I was about to study to be a phlebotomist for free in the hospital, but then discovered that I was pregnant with Emanuel.

When I was 3 months pregnant, my husband was working at Sears as a Mechanic. He got angry with me and hit me as hard as he could in the middle of my back with his shoes several times and I thought that I would miscarry. The next day while he was at work, I told the owners of the place where we were renting from what had happened, and they drove me to a battered women's shelter called "Safe Place."

My husband tried to find me and contacted a Muslim friend of his that worked for the US Agriculture Department. He helped him find out where I was and then he came to the office and threatened them. They came and arrested him and put him in jail for one day.

I quit my job at Hellen Keller to protect the hospital and filed for divorce by default. My Jewish lawyer suggested for me to hide in another state to where he could not find me. He suggested Little Rock,

Arkansas. I didn't even know where that was but said yes.

I went to a battered women's shelter there, and then to Abba House (Mother Theresa's convent for pregnant women). That is where my 2nd son lived his first month of his life. The Church of the Nazarene helped me move to a duplex, paid for the first month's rent, and furnished some of the house. I did not have a bed and had to sleep on the floor with my baby and Gabriel until I could afford the rest.

I worked for the Health Department as a Nurse's Assistant (private duty). A wonderful couple voluntarily watched my sons while I worked. Eventually, I received section 8 housing and moved to an apartment complex at Baseline and Geyer Springs Road.

This area was controlled by the gang called "Crypts". They were enemies of the gang "Bloods." They fought over territory to where to sell their drugs. There was drive- by shootings at the daycare where I kept my kids, and gang wars, where the police would shoot at gang members, while women would stand out on the porches with their children, trying to prevent the gang members from being shot. I wanted to move but couldn't afford to. I thought I'd never get out of this situation, but then I met Calvin.

Calvin was in the Army National Guard and was a radio minister reading Scripture on KMTL radio in Sherwood, Arkansas. He advertised in the paper that he wanted to date a Christian woman, and I answered his ad. He took me to Fur's Restaurant in North Little Rock, Arkansas. I knew when I first saw him that he'd be my husband.

We dated for 7 months and fell deeply in-love with each other. Calvin asked for my hand in marriage in the First Assemblies of God Church on January 19th, 1997. We were married on February 19th, 1997 at this church. We had a wonderful honeymoon at the Hotze House Bed and Breakfast in Little Rock, Arkansas.

Calvin went on drills for the Army on the weekends. After his drills, on March 23rd, 1997, we all decided to grill and have a picnic at a park in North Little Rock, Arkansas and had a great time. When we packed up to go, it was dark, and the moon was out. We both looked up at the moon and he gave me a kiss. He walked to the truck and I heard my sons playing with Calvin.

Calvin was on the ground when I walked towards him, and my sons thought he was pretending to be dead, so they were throwing gravel at him and laughing trying to get him up. I turned him over and saw a trickle of blood streaming down the edge of his mouth and realized that he was not pretending. I started CPR and my sons waved down a vehicle to call 911. When the ambulance arrived, they pronounced him dead. I was in shock as they drove me to the police station for a report.

He was the love of my life. He was the man I should have married in the first place. He was a Holy Spirit filled man that was on fire for God.

He was called the "Tract Man" because he would pass out religious tracts to whomever he met. He had gotten in trouble one time for mailing tracts and letters to the Generals of the US Army and warned to never do that again. He was bold!

If it was not for Him, I would have not known about the infilling of the Holy Spirit. He taught me that what Paul talked about in the Book of Acts 2: 1-6 about the Day of Pentecost applies for today as well. He asked me, "Do you believe it?" I said, "Yes."

He told me to have my pastor at the Assemblies of God to lay his hands upon me and then ask to be filled with the Holy Spirit. I followed his instructions. Being from the Church of the Nazarene (we don't practice speaking in tongues), I didn't think that that would happen, but I did believe in the Word.

The second my pastor did this, I fell out on the floor, my hands were up in the air, and the pastor's wife instructed me to open my mouth. When I did, I started speaking in unknown tongues. When I closed my eyes, I saw circular waves of light and I felt electricity run up my arms and legs. I also felt my stomach roll as though I was throwing up. I was like this for one whole hour, looking straight up into heaven and praising God. It was awesome! For a couple of days afterwards, the power of God was heavy on me and I could not stop speaking in tongues. My kids thought I had gone totally bonkers. After 4 days, it subsided, but I spoke in tongues many times when I prayed afterwards. I just thank God that I met Calvin and was blessed to spend the time on earth that we had together. There is nothing more precious to know that you have been equally yoked with a believer that loves God.

Romans 8:28 – "And we know that all things work together for good to them that know God, to them who are called according to His purpose." (KJV)

I am now a licensed science and generalist teacher for the State of Texas and have recently graduated with my Master of Arts in Theology from Southwestern Assemblies of God University. I hope to use these skills to teach and do missions work in the Middle East. My oldest son Gabriel is an English teacher and my youngest son Emanuel is a registered nurse. They were raised in the church and have accepted Christ as children but need prayer to regain their trust in God.

I believe in the Word that "Train up a child in the way he should go: and when he is old, he will not depart from it." (Proverbs 22:6, KJV) Please be in continual prayer for me and my sons. Praises be to God almighty for bringing us out of terrible situations, and let it be Thy will for us to serve You in any way that Your heart desires, Amen.

# BIBLIOGRAPHY

The Old Souk, Aleppo. Above in 2007 and below in 2013. Photographs: Corbis, Stanley Greene/Noor/Eyevine

https://en.wikipedia.org/wiki/Beheading_of_St._John_the_Baptist

http://www.newworldencyclopedia.org/entry/John_the_Baptist

www.ingramcontent.com/pod-product-compliance
Ingram Content Group UK Ltd.
Pitfield, Milton Keynes, MK11 3LW, UK
UKHW041924190726
13854UKWH00003B/1424

9 781387 539345